D1543384

ANTIBULLYING Clubs

Addy Ferguson

PowerKiDS press.

New York

Published in 2015 by The Rosen Publishing Group, Inc.
29 East 21st Street, New York, NY 10010

First Edition

Editor: Jennifer Way
Book Design: Erica Clendening and Colleen Bialecki
Book Layout: Andrew Povolny
Photo Research: Katie Stryker

Photo Credits: Cover, pp. 1, 11 Steve Debenport/E+/Getty Images; p. 4 Ingram Publishing/Thinkstock; p. 5 JHDT Stock Images LLC/Shutterstock.com; p. 6 Twin Design/Shutterstock.com; p. 7 Fuse/Thinkstock; p. 8, 21 Comstock/Stockbyte/Thinkstock; p. 12 monkeybusinessimages/iStock/Thinkstock; p. 13 BananaStock/Thinkstock; p. 14 tmcphotos/Thinkstock; p. 15 Blend Images - KidStock/Brand X Pictures/Getty Images; p. 16 Tracy Whiteside/iStock/Thinkstock; p. 17 Pressmaster/Shutterstock.com; p. 18 Blend Images/Shutterstock.com; p. 19 VBStock/iStock/Thinkstock; p. 22 Kali Nine LLC/E+/Getty Images.

Library of Congress Cataloging-in-Publication Data

Ferguson, Addy.
 Antibullying clubs / by Addy Ferguson. — First Edition.
    pages cm. — (Stand up: bullying prevention)
 Includes index.
 ISBN 978-1-4777-6631-6 (library binding) — ISBN 978-1-4777-6885-3 (pbk.) —
ISBN 978-1-4777-6623-1 (6-pack)
 1. Bullying—Prevention. I. Title.
 BF637.B85F466 2015
 302.34'3—dc23
                              2013049342

Manufactured in the United States of America

CPSIA Compliance Information: Batch #WS14PK5: For Further Information contact Rosen Publishing, New York, New York at 1-800-237-9932

Contents

What Is Bullying?

You walk down the hall at your school and see a group of kids standing around another student teasing and making fun of him. Is it bullying? Good-natured teasing or one comment that makes another person feel bad is not bullying. However, if a person gets picked on over and over again, that is bullying.

Friends sometimes tease each other. That's OK as long as everyone is laughing. Teasing becomes bullying when the laughter stops and the teasing keeps going.

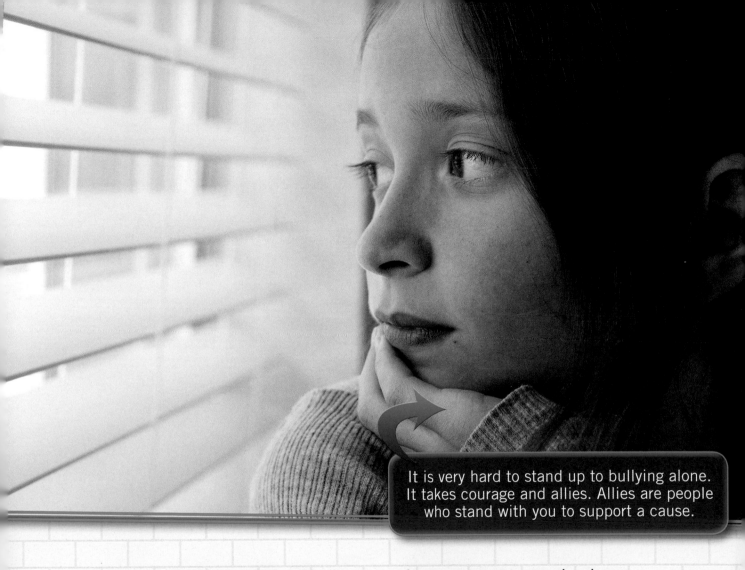

It is very hard to stand up to bullying alone. It takes courage and allies. Allies are people who stand with you to support a cause.

If you have been bullied or you know someone who has, you may have felt powerless to stop it. There are things that you can do to stop bullying, though. Some schools have formed antibullying clubs. These are student clubs that help promote a bully-free atmosphere at school.

Different Kinds of Bullying

You might think that there is only one way to bully. There are many ways a person can bully, though. Some are verbal bullies. They use hateful language and name-calling to hurt another person. Others are **physical** bullies, using force to **intimidate** or hurt another person.

When you think of bullying, you might first picture physical bullies. There are several other ways to bully, though.

Cyberbullies use computers to reach their targets by emails, instant messages, or social networks.

Social bullies convince other people to join in bullying another person. They may **exclude** that person from groups, games, or activities. There is also cyberbullying, in which people use the Internet or **social media** to tease or taunt another person. Every kind of bullying is equally wrong and has the potential to hurt someone badly.

Creating Bully-Free Zones

Some schools have begun programs to help put a stop to bullying. They have declared their hallways and playgrounds bully-free zones. This cannot happen without the support of the entire school community, though. Students, teachers, and everyone else at the school must agree to keep a lookout for bullying and be willing to stand up and stop it.

These antibullying programs do not only focus on stopping bullying that is happening. They also have workshops and discussions at which they **role-play** social situations. These activities are meant to help students understand why bullying is wrong and to prevent them from doing it at all.

Teachers can help make hallways bully free by monitoring them between classes. Hallways are one of the places at school where bullying is most likely to happen.

What Are Antibullying Clubs?

Students in a school may decide to form a club to stop bullying. An antibullying club is a great way to raise awareness of the bullying problem. These clubs are also a great way to show other students that they can stand up to bullying, too. One voice is good. Just think how much better and more powerful it can be to join many voices together.

There are many websites that provide tips and information on how to start an antibullying club in your school or community. The first step is finding a few friends who want to start one with you.

The website for the National Association of People Against Bullying (NAPAB) is one place where you can find information about starting an antibullying club.

Why Do People Bully?

Some bullies have trouble with their schoolwork. This makes them feel helpless, and bullying makes them feel powerful and in control.

Why do some people bully? Some people bully because they like to feel powerful. They choose a target who seems weaker than they are and then use that **imbalance** of power to hurt that person. Other people bully because they feel bad about their own lives. They may have been bullied themselves. Bullying someone else helps them feel more in control.

If you know someone who is being bullied, invite her to join you in starting a club. You don't have to ask her to talk about the bullying. She might want to share anyway, though. You can work together on ways to fix the problem.

Bullies often target kids who are smaller than they are because they feel sure that they can beat them in a fight or that they will not fight back.

Who Gets Bullied?

Anyone can be bullied, but often bullies choose to bully children who do not fit in or who seem different from other students. They may choose a child who is shy. They may choose a child who does better in school or someone who wears different clothing from everyone else. Often children who have physical, emotional, or mental challenges can be targets for bullies, too.

Kids who are very interested in math or science are sometimes targeted by bullies.

Antibullying clubs can help all these types of people. They could put up posters celebrating differences. They could present a skit talking about why it is OK to be different and that no one deserves to be bullied.

Kids with disabilities are more likely to be bullied than other kids.

Long-Term Effects

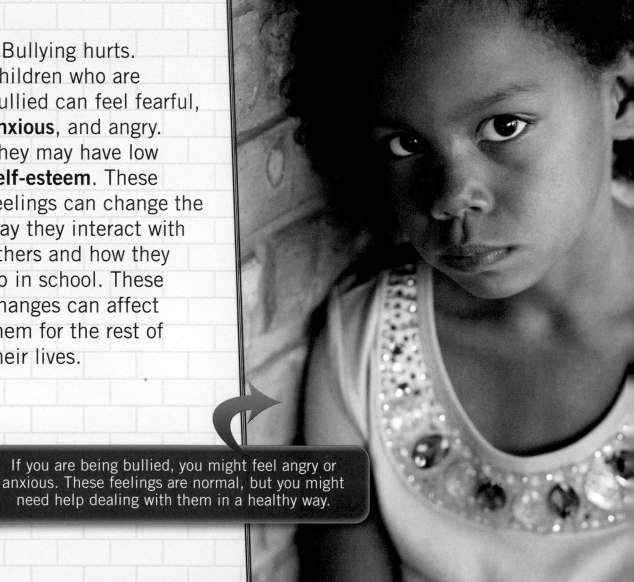

Bullying hurts. Children who are bullied can feel fearful, **anxious**, and angry. They may have low **self-esteem**. These feelings can change the way they interact with others and how they do in school. These changes can affect them for the rest of their lives.

If you are being bullied, you might feel angry or anxious. These feelings are normal, but you might need help dealing with them in a healthy way.

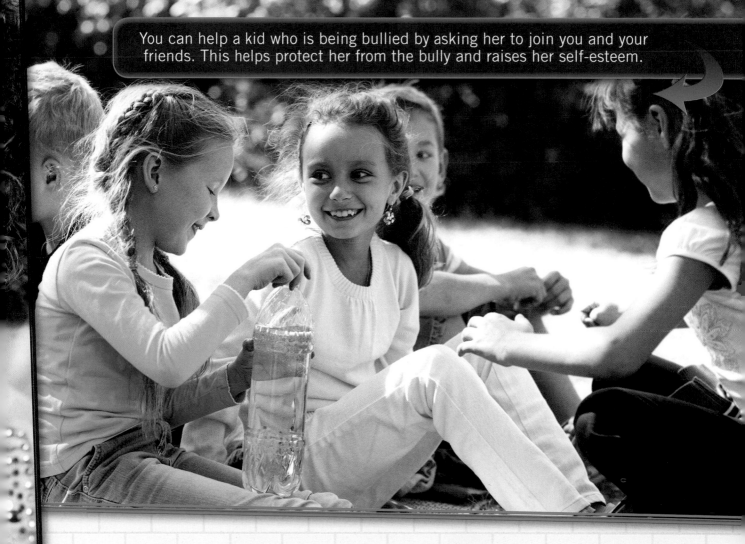

You can help a kid who is being bullied by asking her to join you and your friends. This helps protect her from the bully and raises her self-esteem.

Kids in antibullying clubs can help by inviting the bullied person to join their club. Feeling included goes a long way toward making that person feel better. Antibullying clubs should have trusted adult advisers who can help them, too. This person can give advice and support to children who are bullied.

Standing Together

One of the reasons that bullying has become such a problem is because people look on, but they do nothing to help. People who see bullying happen but do not take part are called **bystanders**.

Antibullying clubs encourage kids to be witnesses who speak out against bullying.

By doing nothing, bystanders are doing the wrong thing because they are allowing bullying to happen.

Antibullying clubs can inspire people to become **witnesses**. Witnesses are people who speak out about what they see. They lend a hand or get help. It can be hard to stand up against a bully alone. Forming a club lets people stand together, and that is a powerful tool against bullying.

Adult Advisers

With any bullying situation, it is important to talk to a trusted adult about it. Get teachers or staff at your school to become advisers of your club. They can help your group come up with ideas about how to spread the word that bullying is wrong. They can also talk to bullied kids and help them find the support they need.

Your group might want to raise funds, through a bake sale or other event, so that you can have an antibullying speaker come to your school. An adult adviser could help you with your planning.

The teacher who is the adviser for a school's antibullying club can also talk to bullies.

Ending Bullying

Every day, somewhere in this country, someone will be bullied. This sad fact won't change unless more people watch for signs of bullying and try to stop it.

Forming or joining an antibullying club is one way to make our schools and neighborhoods safe for everyone. No one deserves to be bullied, no matter what. It is up to you to take the first step toward making your school a bully-free zone.

You can be the person who brings your school community together to make your school a bully-free zone.

Glossary

anxious (AYNK-shus) Uneasy or worried.

bystanders (BY-stan-derz) People who are there while something is taking place but are not taking part in what is happening.

exclude (eks-KLOOD) To keep or shut someone out.

imbalance (im-BA-lunts) The state of being unequal.

intimidate (in-TIH-muh-dayt) To make shy or afraid.

physical (FIH-zih-kul) Having to do with the body.

role-play (ROHL-PLAY) To act out.

self-esteem (SELF-uh-STEEM) Happiness with oneself.

social media (SOH-shul MEE-dee-uh) Online communities through which people share information, messages, photos, videos, and thoughts.

witnesses (WIT-nes-ez) People who watch an action or event.

Index

Websites

Due to the changing nature of Internet links, PowerKids Press has developed an online list of websites related to the subject of this book. This site is updated regularly. Please use this link to access the list: www.powerkidslinks.com/subp/clubs/